Into Light

Poems By

Lee Underwood

Photograpy credits:
Front cover (reading a book): Michael Costa
Back cover (sitting and playing guitar): Bryce Tyson

ISBN: 978-1-63649-698-6

Poetic Matrix Press
www.poeticmatrix.com

Into Light

INTRODUCTION

Nearly all of these poems were written in 2020, the year in which covid-19 moved from China, to Europe, to the United States—an amazing series of movements that changed our lives. Infections. Deaths. Face masks, distancing, personal isolation. Racial protests. Civic chaos. Global instability.

The burdens were great, and still are—the lingering deleterious effects of Trump's corrupt administration and his non-functioning Senate. The covid-19 pandemic. The plummeting economy. The horrideous psychological diminution of confidence, energy, will power, and creative courage throughout the land.

Nevertheless, in spite of these and related burdens, the center of the human heart remains forever alive. We love, we care, we doubt, we fear. We scale the heights in our mind, sometimes succeed, sometimes fail, and always aspire to realize the best, the most hopeful, the most loving and empathic dimensions of ourselves. That is what most of these poems are about: the forever-shining jewel-center of the universal human heart.

There are a few angry poems in this book, but not many. The emphasis is definitely not on the ambitious, political, power-seeking, greed-driven acquisitive sides of our selves. In the main, these poems emerge from the heartsong center of who we truly are. We care. We hope and doubt. And yes, we yearn to love and be loved. Indeed, our empathic caring for others is the foundation upon which humanity seeks both its fulfillment and its redemption.

Where in the center of it all do we find ourselves? Alone? We are not alone. We are not isolated. Even when feeling alone, we remain together as one. Even when feeling alone in our thoughts, fears, hopes and yearnings, we are sweet-close, heart-close with all others who surround us in our house, in our neighborhoods, and throughout the rest of the world. Sometimes we know this. Sometimes we don't. Nevertheless, the truth remains.

Let us close our eyes, allow ourselves to slip into a moment of inner silence. For that moment let us transcend our daily demands, miseries, considerations and move into the sweet purity of our own selfless inner quietude. Into those moments in which we allow our thoughts and personal hurts, pains, and fears to disappear. Let us welcome the opening into quietude, into the thoughtless riverrun, the stream in the mountains that asks no questions.

* * * *

In section I, "Beyond The Breakers" is a metaphor. It is a state of mind and being, beyond the waves crashing on the shore. Beyond the noise, pollution and chaos of contemporary civilization, beyond the competition, the ambition, the storms, tears, misery and rages of modernity.

Out beyond the breakers is a quiet place, far out at sea, where the waters are clean, clear and calm; the spaciousness is vast; the sky is a cloudless deep blue. It is a place in the heart and the mind that is forever with us, accessible whenever we choose to go there within ourselves, into quietude.

When I say "Into Light" in Section II, I am again speaking metaphorically. It is that place within where thoughts have stilled, where a sense of beatitude predominates, a place, not of literal light, but a heartsong place of mental and physical wholeness and well-being—the psycho-spiritual light of the soul, the metaphorical light, the sense of inner illumination that mystics and highly evolved spiritual beings have been telling us about for millennia.

* * * *

At the age of 82, I have no answers about a God in the sky or a heavenly afterlife. In my poem "I Don't Know Much About God, But . . ." I express the notion that there is only one Cosmic energy, expressed in an infinity of forms. I rather like the Zen idea that everything is everything else.

So, although I adhere to no theological or ideological position, I have led a full life and have explored myself and others quite thoroughly. These poems are sparks from that life-journey.

I have ridden in airplanes, but have no desire to pilot one. I have ridden in 18-wheeler trucks, but have no desire to own one. I have visited wealthy homes but have no desire to purchase one. Indeed, I have never been ambitious, but have in my own fashion accomplished numerous things that have touched the hearts and minds of at least a few people, and which directly or indirectly inform the writings in this book.

As a youth I was a high school football running-back and something of a track star. I graduated from San Francisco State College and briefly attended UC Berkeley graduate school. I hitch-hiked across the USA during my "Kerouac" period; rode a bicycle through much of England and France; and hitch-hiked in Spain, meeting and talking with Salvador Dali on the Mediterranean beach outside his home in Cadaques, and meeting and talking with Hemingway at the bull fights in Barcelona and Valencia.

I have body-surfed the waves of the Pacific Ocean; camped and fly fished in the Rocky Mountains of Colorado; and hiked back country trails in Utah, Colorado and New Mexico. I have also known several women well; have drunk too much on more than one occasion; spent ten years in psychotherapy; and have been happily married to my dear wife Sonia Crespi for more than 45 years.

As well, I have played piano and guitar, written and sung my own songs in San Francisco and New York, and toured and recorded as Tim Buckley's lead guitarist for seven years, standing before audiences on stages great and small including Carnegie Hall, Philharmonic Hall, and Madison Square Garden. I interviewed jazz musicians and wrote cover stories as West Coast Editor of *Down Beat* magazine for five years. I have written and read my own poetry in L.A., San Francisco, and New York; and have published two books of poetry—*Timewinds,* (Poetic Matrix Press 2011) and *Diamondfire,* (Outskirts Press, 2016). I have authored a biography of Tim Buckley entitled *Blue Melody: Tim Buckley Remembered* (Backbeat, 2001).

Throughout my years, I have been an avid listener to music of all generic styles and an avid reader of fiction, poetry, psychology, philosophy, and spirituality. Here, in "Gone But Still Singing In My Heartsong," I have listed in a kind of poetic fashion some of the many authors, musicians, artists, scientists, psychologists and spiritual teachers who have transfixed my attention and won my heart.

I bring these and many more experiences to the writing of the poems contained between these covers. It is my deepest wish that you read them with your eyes, your awakened mind, and your singing heart. Meanwhile, I can say I've done the best I could, and wish all well.

READY

Ol' Superjock
Ran his race
Made his touchdowns
Played his music
Wrote his poems
Loved his wife
Chopped his wood
Read his books
    And finally
Packed his bags,
    Ready for the
    Bright-Light
    Flame-Out.

Acknowledgements

Diamondfire, 2016—"Gathering Light," "This Moment," "I Don't Know Much About God," "The Tight-Rope Walker," "The Thinker"

Timewinds, 2010—"Three Eyes," "I Don't Know Much About God"

"I Don't Know Much About God"—"In The Grove," Lee Herrick, editor. "ZamBomba," Paula Shell and Julia Holzer, editors

Into Light

Dedicated to

Sonia Crespi

Love Beauty Joy Compassion

The Soul-mate who has

Been my guiding light

forever

Contents

Into Light

Beyond The Breakers

Into Light

Beyond the Breakers

A Simple Turning of the Page

If I were swept up and away
Into the full moon's shining corona,
There to meet those who are gone
But still singing in my heart-song,
Might you remember me?

Morning walk, eerie quietude—
Silent streets; windows blank;
A woodpecker ratta-tat-tatting;
A distant crow cawing through the fog;
A sparrow bathing in a puddle.

Walking alone beneath a grey sky—
Roses and lilies blossoming;
Front-yard apple trees abloom;
Lemons swelling, nearly ripe now;
Life abundant, except for man.

Those grand poets and authors;
Those dazzling singers and guitarists;
Those magnificent pianists I loved—
Might I join them? Might they
Welcome me as a friend?

And when I, too, am swept up and away
Into the full moon's bright corona,
Might you remember a poetic word of mine,
Maybe a phrase or a sweet melody—
Perhaps a simple turning of the page?

I Still Know the Song

I still know the song my life sings. It dims,
But never disappears. Quietude,
Storms, peaches, pears, lemons,
And freshly picked apples make
All the difference: time stands still forever.

Clear-eyed in these dark covid days,
I remember the spark that lights
My soul, your smile and the hope of the world—
The strength of love and courage that
Makes a new day possible, real, and true.

A woman in Spain reads my words,
Sympathetically vibrates to their music,
Resonates to the melodies and the touch
Of these sweet heartsongs. She makes
All the difference: I am here for her.

I am here as well for those who listen
And hear in these songs the rhythms,
Melodies, and quiet intensity of this
Moment in which I write my soul, offering
Courage, fire, and resounding strength to all.

No time but now. No place but here.
Among family, lovers, friends and
Compatriots, there are no divisions.
Together we stand, we sing, we envision
One world, indivisible, united in love for each and all.

Sing out, yes. Sing loudly and clearly. Sing bravely.
Defy the cruelty and corruption gripping us now;
Embrace our reason (so battered and bruised);
Our noble vision (so desecrated, besmirched);
And the passionate intelligence of our visionary fathers.

America the beautiful has always led the way.
Life, liberty and the pursuit of happiness is not
A catch phrase for venal tv bean commercials—
It is the music of our nation's grand global song.
Forever remember vision, hope, strength, and courage.

Darkness and Light

Such a silly lad am I, watching my mind,
Surveying my words, catching my commas,
Imagining this written phrase might spark
A feeling, a thought, a revolutionary urge
In some sensitive man, some sweet woman,
Some wayward genius sharing this midnight hour.

Who knows where these mind-trips into dreams,
Delicacy, sensuality, true love, memory—
Who knows where they lead? Tantalizing, seductive.
Yes, darkness and light sleep closely together—
We're so often seduced before we know it.
Seduction, yes, is always within our own mind.

I've never known a moment of attraction that did not
Speak to me before I heard it. Always the other became
The me I never knew until they awakened it.
Realization's light came slowly, perhaps reluctantly,
But always I welcomed becoming lost in my own desire.
Giving myself to the other was giving myself to me.

Confessions in the night become time's demise.
Releasing yesterday's grip, we give up tomorrow.
Here-now has such beauty, so colorful, so delightful,
So many tears, hopes, dreams, passions, visions,
Promises, bitter pains. Release memory, release time,
Open your heart, and set this shining moment free.

Another way

All the guns, all the ambition,
    All the need, all the desperation,
All the loss, all the fear,
    All the envy, all the greed,
All the murders of love, integrity, hope,
    Joy, compassion—

Easy to despair, oh yes
    Easy to quit, oh yes,
Easy to give up and
    Fall down in tears.
Easy to embrace cynicism—
    "Nothing will ever change."

And, yes, we feel our heartaches
    Rising and, yes, we shake
Our fists in anger-fire, weeping
    Bitter tears in darkest night,
Burying our face in the pillow,
    Trying to stifle anguish
And our hopeless, helpless sighs—

Easy to despair, oh yes—
Understandable, oh yes . . .

    But no —

There
    Is
        Another
            Way

Can we step back from
        The brink of darkest night?
Can we break the grip of hypnotic dream?
        Can we step away from the cliff's edge
And for a flashing moment remember the best,
        The strongest and the truest in ourselves?

Can we recall and embrace
        The years of climbing to this point?
Can we recall and embrace the struggles
        We endured to become our individual selves?

The bubonic plague of Shakespeare's time,
        The flu epidemic of 1918,
The Hitler War, the Neo-fascist Trump years,
        And the Covid-19 plague of our own time—

All struggles
            Can be met
All struggles
            Can be overcome

Let us stand up and let us stand tall,
        Awake, proud, united with all,
Touching
        Hands,
                Touching
                        Hearts

Let us sing our heartsongs
        And rise up
                on spirit's wings
                        To shining light—

Bless the troubadours,
Bless the poets,
Bless the artists and writers,
Bless strength and compassion,
Bless love and nature—
Bless the
Power of beauty
Bless the
Power of music—

Yes, let singing souls
Forever arise in our midst
And give themselves to
Love and tomorrow's promise—

Above all, let us celebrate the human heart
With its joysmiles and abject tears,
With its infinite, unbounded capacity
To rise,
And to rise still again
To that light
That shines
Within us all—

Stand quietly now,
Let us close our eyes,
Still our mind
Open our hearts,
And listen closely—

Listen...
And hear
The music
Of those
Celestial choirs
Singing forever

Remember the Singing

Something sad,
And yet so beautiful
In the awesome destruction
Of our planet and our time—

And so I sing . . .
Not for myself alone,
But for all of our sweet
Lives on earth—

Deer in the forests
Cats in the jungles
Birds in the trees
For all of our furry and feathered friends,
So wild, so innocent, so vulnerable.

Even as we watch the
Madness billowing, cascading,
The earth-wrenching twists of our lives,
The unbelievable descent into psychosis,
Desperation, homelessness,
Dying, death, and mass graves—
Even in these howling moments—

Dolphins returning to Venice;
Smog lifting from the Himalayas;
Skies clearing over the Rockies
Poppies, roses and apple trees
Blooming and swaying in the wind . . .

I seek only your heart,
My silent melodies shining
In these words,
Alive and singing—

Listen, yes
And do not despair—
Remember the song,
Remember the singing,
Even as I remember you
In each moment's melody.

Yesterdays are Gone

All those yesterdays behind my eyes
Sparkled and danced,
Laughed and dreamed so vividly—
High school football, early piano,
First love, and the colorful places
I lived in—Colorado, Texas,
northern New York, Washington, D.C.

College, beer, sex,
Jazz piano, and new places, too—
Rocky Mountains, San Francisco—
Riding a bicycle to school
Along the Pacific Coast Highway;
Graduating, teaching, learning guitar,
Married, divorced, on the loose again.

The Tim Buckley years — guitar in hand,
Greenwich Village, Santa Monica Civic,
Philharmonic Hall, Carnegie Hall;
Recording studios, sex, drugs, rock 'n' roll,
Home in Venice at the beach,
Love once again, then over, gone . . .

These memories and a thousand more
Crowded my mind so often for so many years,
Even when I outgrew them and moved into a new now
That brought me true love, marriage 40+ years,
Hundreds of great books, dazzling authors—
Hemingway, Kerouac, Hermann Hesse,
Osho, Krishnamurti, T'ao Ch'ien, so many more . . .

My yesterdays rode with me in those memories
Just behind my eyes when dozing off to sleep,
Flashing through my daytime thoughts,
Drifting in my mind even in conversation—

And now? Where is my history now?
A new day, a new time, a new slate,
A new life for me, yes,
And for the whole world—

Our yesterdays are gone, forever gone.
There is no "normal" as we once knew it,
No turn of the screw or pounding of the nail,
No clever formula, no quick fix,
No unifying thought, creed, philosophy,
No book, map, compass, or savior.
Our personal and collective histories
Are over, done with, finished,
Vanished into history's gaping maw.
Dreams, memories and language have
Disappeared into a soul-night darkness,
Into a blank stare that has no mirror,
A frightened yowl that has no echo.

The realization seizes us suddenly:
No past, no glistening hope,
No wisdom-words, and no tomorrow.
Staring up at the night-sky,
We can no longer see the stars.
A new moment greets us,
A new identity, a new reality,
Wordless, silent, faceless,
Thoughtless, lethal,
And beyond comprehension . . .

Let there be light
In sprigs of bright grasses
Sprung up from dry surfaces
Into a world of health,
Hope, strength, joy,
And new leaves,
Shining in the mid-day sun.

Let deer find paths
Through urban alleys;
Let fish find clean waters
In high seas beyond the breakers;
Let birds find safe havens
In unbroken, unscarred forests;
And, yes, let there be light once more
Where darkness once blinded us
With its merciless shades
And impenetrable shadows.

Clarity

Are you ready
To meet a stillness
You have never known before?
Pristine quietude,
No names, no labels,
No streaming images, no words—

Autumn leaves
Red, gold, yellow, orange,
Cool mist on cheeks,
A lone bird winging south . . .

Mind open,
Still and quiet,
Radiant and
Clear within;
Clear without . . .

Wordless spaciousness,
Seeing without language,
Direct perception—

A vast and cloudless
Deep blue mind-sky

Baggage

They call it "baggage."
We carry it with us—
Old songs, new songs,
Mist, feathers, dew drops,
Spring flowers, autumn leaves,
Heartaches, night sobs, tears.

Faces remembered, faces forgotten,
Loved ones, enemies, buddies,
Girlfriends, boyfriends, mad ones,
Things told to us, things we said,
Things we tried to say but couldn't.
Echoing hallways, distant laughter.

Not easy, caring, not caring,
Wishing we cared, trying to care.
No resolution, no finality,
Endless chatter, streaming images,
Nothing, something, not much,
High school laughter, muttering ghosts.

Flux, change, spinning,
Rising, falling, waves, troughs—
And in the end, an open space,
Vast, empty, benevolent,
Strange, quiet, suspended,
Not old, new, but oddly familiar . . .

When air stills and the sun dips,
Yesterdays and tomorrows

Dissolve, disappear . . . And lo—
A vibrant instant becomes forever,
Planets, suns and stars become
A cosmos of connections—

Gleaming, resplendent,
Shining, soaring, merging,
Swirling, whirling, blazing—

Yes, only yes, forever yes

The eternal moment: one

The pulsing heart of the rose.

Many in One

Can you remember
The ways in which
Our doubts and fears
And desperate dreams
Bring us together?

In our madness
Our isolation
And nervous tremblings
We are not alone.

Sing, to remember,
Sing, to enliven,
Sing, to sound your love,
Your hope, and your sense
Of you-me, we-us-together—

One in many,
        Many in one

Those Musketeers
        Were right . . .

Riversong

Love in all ways

Yes, too, and yes,
Song of light,
Sweet our kiss,
And closely hold me,
Fingers touching,
Touching sweetly,
Slowly touching
Free me. . . No time . . .
Timeless . . .

In your own forgetting,
Keep me with you—
Yes,
Our sweet
Riversong

Remember, yes,
The aching, yearning,
Smiles
Singing in our eyes,
Our yes-me-love,
So warm, so human,
So radiantly human
In our forever
Riversong—

Universal light

The Sound of Love

And so I seek and search
For a silver bell
Among the offerings,
A glance, a smile,
A token of who I am

Feels so good'
To find a flower,
A pussycat,
An occasional song,
A smile among the sufferings

Who might I be?
No matter—
Once here . . . Once gone

Yes, my heart
Sings for all of us
Here, now, in this
Strange, beautiful,
Horrifying moment,
A time perhaps
Of Earth's return to
Clear streams, singing aspens,
Pristine air, and quietude.

Here we are—
Sing me a quiet melody,
Bear with me in my tremblings
I am with you in my love
I am with you in my
    Heartsong . . .

Be with me now,
Hold me close
You are my silver bell
I am the sound of love . . .

In the Moment Now

Our past is a long-gone dream
Our memories but balms,
Blankets, tranquilizers,
Sweet intoxicants, escapes
Dearly and direly needed

Yes, but . . .

We are in the moment now
Horrific scenes, a sci-fi movie,
Yes, but not a fantasy,
Not make-believe,
Not a dream, and
Nowhere to get away . . .

So what to do?
        run?
        hide?
        why not?
Embrace yesterday?
        dive into alcohol?
        get lost in sex, drugs,
        the magic of music?

Yes, oh, yes, I need
My dreams away from now;
I need my touch, my sounds,
My swirling images of
Sex, fire and beauty,

The saving-savior presence
Of impassioned forgetfulness,
Yes, please, oh yes, please release me . . .

But we are in the moment now . . .

No Need for Tears

In a midnight dream, standing on a hill overlooking
The river winding below, trees along the banks,
Slow winds blowing leaves from side to side,
I recall a hundred thou's, a thousand moments,
A million hugs, kisses, promises, hopes, daydreams.

Yes, some blossomed into lilies and roses,
And yes, some brought waking joy to me;
Some held my hand in gentle sympathy,
And yes, some also wept with each
Heartbeat coursing through my veins.

How my songs sing these aching nights, awake,
Alone, wondering again the ways of time and joy,
The ways they merge, dissolve, transform.
Some joys sparkle, and fuel sweet words that
Welcome flirtatious eyes and wandering hands.

Sorrows too remain, sometimes snarling beneath
Dark currents, calm on the surface, roiling below
In darkness dimly lit by fading midnight suns.
Where are you, father? You did all you could to help.
Where are you, mother? Smiling, dancing, caring.

The rule was suits, ties, short hair, degrees, contacts.
Never something like a father beating his daughter,
Desiring her, needing her, and hating her because of it.
Nothing worthy of novels, poetry, dramatic films.
A conventional life, proper values, guidelines, conduct.

Standing on a hill overlooking the valley river below,
Prosaic miseries float back in dreams, along with loves
That once flamed then died of age, stealing away the
Joys and passion and laughter we once had. Nothing
Unusual, nothing unique, just love of love, of life and time.

What can one say? After our final sigh, moons
Drift behind clouds, and clouds bring rain. Songs
Once so glorious fade like grainy films. Babies
Gurgle and laugh and flash bright smiles that last
A day or so . . . No need for tears. No need for tears.

Keep the Music Singing

Statistics are horrideous—
Absorb them, yes, but
Do not let them define
The who-you-are—

How to transcend?

The daily news is a love-drug—
Gets you now, gets you quick,
Sweet-talks you in,
Tricks you, yes—
How resist the pull, the tug,
The instant descent
Into voluptuous depression?

Empathy is no excuse—
Love thy neighbor, yes,
But do not let the numbers
Abuse you, crack you, reduce you
To weeping wasteland ashes.

Gentle detachment—
Not indifference;
Love with compassionate
Connection, not fear.
Keep the music singing
        In your soul,
        Your heartsong,
        Your questing mind . . .

You are so beautiful—
Don't let them maim you . . .

Roofs and Foundations

When the foundation is not cast,
The walls cannot be built;
When walls cannot be built
The roof cannot spread its protection.

When those who sing of the roof
Deny those who build foundations,
The building collapses.

And when those who build foundations
Sneer at those who envision the roof,
Only empty wastelands surround us . . .

Eons

Some said he got lost in the ethers
    wasn't practical, didn't know
    how to pay bills, make appointments,
    file taxes, plant trees, build houses,
    earn a living, cope with computers,
    money, contracts, telephone calls

Some said he was bright, others said
    he was not exactly realistic,
    accurate, quick, or talkative,
    but he did have a nice smile
    a sort of charming affability,
    a way of speaking that felt safe

He usually woke early, sat a while,
    leaned into candlelight
    sipped his coffee, wrote a poem
    (or two or three) that nobody read.
    he didn't mind, just scribbled awhile,
    set them aside until the pages grew

When he died, people wondered who he was,
    what he said, what he did, but
    few really knew, and nobody really cared.
    they slid him into a furnace, propped his ashes
    in a jar on a shelf and went their way—
    time flowed on, moons passed, suns burned

Grasses sprouted, lemons ripened,
geese flew, rivers flowed—
somebody found a box of poems
in an attic, published them,
nobody noticed, the world spun on,
new generations sprang up, danced, died off

Mountains emerged, forests flowered,
civilizations burgeoned, making lots of noise;
books, films, music glittered, strutted, vanished;
buildings crumbled, new ones soared high;
every word, thought, feeling twirly-whirled, disappeared
and, lo, within change, nothing changed at all

Somebody once said, "No meaning out there,"
meaning, "Look within," and yet hardly anybody looked,
maybe one or two, and they were deemed "crazy."
"So what?" Someone said. "Don't care," someone else said.
A bang? A whimper? A sigh? A teardrop? Maybe two?
Mystery? Meaning? Philosophy, politics, religion?

Nothing there. No place to go. Nobody knows.
But, wait—what about the dance, the sweet kiss,
The kind word, the friendly gesture, the helping hand?
What about love, compassion, creativity?
Maybe . . .   Maybe . . .
Meanwhile, stars keep on gleaming,
lovers keep on dancing,
And the world and its ways keep on keepin' on . . .

The Canoe Rider

Just a fellow riding his canoe
Down the river toward the falls,
Noting the banks on either side—

The bank of Yes, the bank of No;
The bank of White, the bank of Black;
The bank of Day, the bank of Night.

No shaggy mountain-top guru;
No high-hatted Catholic priest;
No red-robed Buddhist chanter;

Just a wandering musician-poet;
Enjoying the waters, the sun, the light;
The river he rides uniting both banks as One.

Universal gesture

Beautiful breasts,
Soft flowing hair,
Open arms,
Beckoning eyes
So dark, so alive—

Tongue-tip lips,
Ready, eager, open,
Waiting for
The sweet embrace,
The universal gesture—
. . .Yes . . .

So Strange

Profoundly alone
We reach out,
Knowing our
Boundaries,
Limitations,
History,

    Doubts—

So strange,
The moment of caring

    And yet,
    And yet . . .

Alone, isolated
Within the scope of
Mind-stream memories,
The way we were . . .
We anxiously embrace
Connections, loved ones,
Sweet songs, smiles,
Laughter, touches—

    Melodies recalled,
Images vivid,
And yet here-now,
Heartsong close . . .

I love you
In remembrance
So holy,
My heart quakes—
You are with me now . . .
          No time . . .
We are each other's dream.

Solitude

Are we but a dot
Confined within
Our own skull?
Are we simply
Contained alone
Inside a room
Within a city block?
Are we but lonely
Solitary body-minds
Isolated inside
Neighborhoods and
Other peoples' lives,
Surrounded by
Trees, mountains,
The sky, the stars,
A dark and yawning universe?

Perhaps we can be more—
Perhaps we can awaken,
Sitting before a candle's
Wavering flame
Peaceful, serene,
Without dream-stream
Memories, thoughts,
Concepts, fears,
Hopes, doubts,
Anxieties, ambitions . . .

Could this be?

Maybe solitude
Is not isolation at all.
Maybe we can be
Completely present,
Alive, alert, awake

With clear minds,
Relaxed, present, serene,
Open, unbounded,
Transparent, expansive,
Embracing all that is.

Can we be fully human,
Fully awakened beings
Generating and releasing
The mind, the body,
The room, the neighborhood,
The trees, the mountains,
The sky, the stars, and, yes,
The infinite universe beyond?

Maybe solitude is
Not isolation at all—
Not an aching loneliness
Yearning for the Other, but
A centered, vibrant presence,
In which the endless past
And the endless future
Are ecstatically embraced
And joyously set free
Within timeless nows
All-inclusive Eternal Moment

Singing for the Now

Wish I could sing a song of love
    wish I could sing a song of light
Wish I could touch the hearts
    of all who live here in my time
And live in all times to come . . .

Vanity, vanity, vanity, my friend—
    just sing your song of love,
Your song of clear mountain light,
    your song of gentle laughter, yes,
And let the times do whatever they like.

Those who have ears to hear will hear;
    the deaf and dumb will not.
Those who have eyes to see will read;
    the blind will forever remain alone.
Just love, sing, share, smile, and wave farewell.

Then, Now

Ah, yes, those youthful days
When innocence and anguish
Danced a joyful/tearful dance—

Marlon Brando's wild one,
James Dean's pouty one,
Kerouac's wacky one—

They sang their brave,
Sweet passion-songs,
And, yes, I heard them.

Through these agéd eyes
I still see them glimmering,
Laughing, drinking, searching.

And, yes, I still love them,
But from a distance and
In a different way—

The air is thinner now;
The views are grander;
Love is sweeter;

And time is beautiful in its
Passing moments—
Smooth, quiet, shining . . .

Toward the Edge

Amazing, watching our human madness—
Some would call it chaos, others a circus;
Some would call it insanity, others folly.

It's an aberrant spectacle with its
Violent rage, wild-eyed fear,
Insatiable greed, ruthless ambition, and
Desperate clutchings, grabbings, lungings.

Our human condition writhes in apprehension—
The covid plague, a plummeting economy,
Systemic racism, cops murdering blacks,
A narcissistic psychopath in high office—
Passion without compassion;
Anger without reason;
Loyalty without insight;
And no sign of love, quietude or mercy.

How I long for quiet breezes whispering
Among pines and dancing aspens;
For clear mountain streams tumbling down
Untouched canyons into crystalline lakes.
A natural life, rooted in earth, attuned with stars.

I long, as well, to feel the pulse of a cat's purr,
And hear the swirl and surge of music attuned with life;
To witness a baby snuggling in its mother's arms,
Or an agéd father embracing his son for the last time.

Rages have their passions;
Eruptions have their volcanoes;
Fires have their forests;
Storms have their oceans.
Humans, too, rise up in fury,
Ambition, fear, outraged pride—
And curse their neighbors,
Wound their children,
Slaughter their enemies, and
Break their loved one's heart.

Yes, we all wish for change,
But change cannot come with
Insatiable pride; fear of others;
Lust for power; heartless greed;
And the self-centeredness of
Me, Mine, and More . . .

And so we ride onward toward the edge—
The blind thinking they see clearly;
The deaf believing they hear;
The calloused touting feelings;
The exhausted dreaming strength;
The mad claiming sanity;
The miserable drinking poison;
The ambitious shouting "Higher!";
The losers boasting victory;
The cruel laughing at affliction.

Oh, the sorrows wrought upon us
By our demented annihilators
And their ruthless, insidious cunning.

Sing a song of quiet ocean breezes, my friend.
A song of bright summer beaches;
A song of dancing aspens and
A clear mountain morning.

Above all,
Sing a song of tender love
That's strong and unafraid,
A song of courage and joy
For thyself and all who know
And understand these words.

And let these words ring true, as well,
Throughout the land in every human heart.

Journey-Song

He galloped through his youth
Riding a proud stallion, tossing poems,
Laughing, dancing, kissing the girls,
Strumming his guitar and singing songs.

The sun shone brightly, mountain streams
answered his call, ocean waves danced,
Star River sparkled in an infinite sky,
summer rains showered flowers in his wake.

His beard turned frosty blue, his hair snow-white,
his muscles ached, but he kept on singing.
let music be my heartsong's guide, he cried.
soon enough I'll leap again, be gone.

When night enfolds my smile and I become
a distant memory, let music-streams sing on;
let new poems whirly-jig in moonlight, and
new children dance their joyful passions wild.

THE SOUND OF SILENCE

Blank white page, eyes closed,
Evening dusk, quiet in the studio,
Quiet in the mind, emotions still,
Heart relaxed, open, receptive . . .

Waiting not for images, memories,
Events, or waterfall emotions;
Simply waiting, receptive,
Listening to the silence of
Inner emptiness, spaciousness,
Unfragmented wholeness . . .

From outside, a distant car,
A breeze rustling trees;
From inside, a sustained,
High-pitched body-tone,
Faint, almost inaudible,
A thin, unwavering line
Spanning the mind-space—
The sound of silence.

Personal hopes, regrets, no;
Obsessions, preoccupations, no;
Individual aspirations, no;
Social concerns, no;
Dreams, memories, fantasies, no;
Thoughts, ideas, concepts, no.

Sitting still in all-embracing
Quietude; wholeness complete;
All-encompassing presence
Imbued with compassion;
Benevolent acceptance in
The love and beauty of all that is.

In the midst of modernity
And its chaotic momentum,
No past, future, no struggle—
Just here, in this timeless moment,
Complete, whole, imbued with light,
Embraced within the spacious mind,
Attuned with the sound of silence.

Who Were We Then?

Who were we then?
What drew us together?
Were we currents mingling
In blue air, or spring clouds
Dancing in a joyous whirlwind?

I feel older these days,
Changing slowly, like a tree.
We made light between us,
Exchanging sparks, our eyes bright,
As we twirled through our time.

Our laughter rang down hallways—
Who were we? Younger, yes,
Less like trees, more like blondes,
Brunettes, red heads, pin-up posters.
All was well, then things changed.

Clothes changed, smiles changed,
Hair styles changed, movies changed,
And suddenly we found ourselves
In other people's lives, smiling,
Laughing, hugging, kissing.

Once in a while looking back now—
A little blurry, sometimes blank,
Often a mere glimpse, recalling
A particular tingle in the laugh,
A quirky smile, a word, a funny gesture.

All my yesterdays sing in gratitude
For the music we made and our dance,
For the sweet touch cheek to cheek,
For the remembered laughter that's always here,
For all you lovingly gave that still remains.

A Very Personal Matter

First things first—
Gotta pick a place. Where?
Motel? Parking lot? Home?
Livingroom, bathroom, bedroom?

Options, options, options.
A lotta history. Lotta motives.
Lotta methods, advantages,
Disadvantages, possibilities,
Fears, considerations, decisions . . .

Why wait? Why not wait?
What about loved ones?
What about scrapbooks,
Memories, wills, goodbye notes,
Histories of the many lives I've led?
Sons, daughters, cousins, friends—
What about all those others?
Vanity? (shame, shame, shame)
Love? (vanity, vanity, vanity)

Nobody carries friends, relatives,
Stocks, bonds, savings,
Scrapbooks, libraries, recordings,
Sons, daughters, cousins,
Or memories to the grave.
This is, after all, a very personal matter.

Alone is a common condition among
Singers, songwriters, drinkers,
Poets, druggies, writers,
All who rise above the fray
And don't mind solitude—
A recluse knows a
Different kind of alone.
Free, relaxed, not aching for
Love, understanding, the Other.
Alone is the most dramatically personal,
The most vivid, lovely, spectacular,
Tender, touching, and relevant
Personal matter of all, in fact,
Especially when considering
The roaring orange flames
Of the burning ghats.

So the question of if and when
Becomes more a question of
Choices, methods, and style.
Ahh, yes, style. Style matters.
Results are the same:
Dead is dead—no need for
Tears, fears or cheers.
It's about how you do it. And what
They say about it afterwards, right?

Could fly to Bangkok, for example.
Rent a room, strip naked,
Step into a closet,
Tie a noose to the bar,
Loop it around my neck,

Get hot, excited, hard, strong,
Kick out the stool, drop sharply,
Commit *autoerotic asphyxiation*.
Actor david carradine did that.
Autoerotic asphyxiation.
What a great name—
Autoerotic asphyxiation.
Would look so cool
Fading out on a tombstone
As the weeds grew all around
And nobody cared any more.
But, alas, it makes for bad reviews.
Everybody just laughs.

Or i could get good and drunk,
No holding back, staggering,
Slurring, maybe falling about,
Crawl across the floor to bed,
Open a full bottle of Vodka ,
Drink it all, swallow a vial of Oxycodone,
And watch the shades and shadows
Descend like voluptuous midnight clouds—
And let blackest night and total oblivion
Drop like a hammer on my forehead,
Slam-bamming eyes shut forever.
Chanteuse Amy Winehouse did that.
Reviews were great. And record sales soared.

Drowning has its attractions, too, especially the bliss.
Swimming out beyond the breakers on my back,
Dark-blue sky above, black water below.
Shore-lights twinkling far away.
Turning over, diving gracefully down into the

Cool darkness of summer's night-ocean,
Water moving sensually about my body,
Filling lungs smoothly, quietly, easily,
No coughing, like inhaling air.
Consciousness dimming, memories slowing,
Heartaches easing, all those failures,
Losses, humiliations going, going—
Sweet calm descending, quiet now,
Midnight blue phasing into perfect silence . . .

Then, of course, there is always the gun.
Quicker than liquor and accurate, for sure.
What kind? Where? How?
A revolver, a .38 Special. Small. Easy in the hand.
Not complicated. Familiar in the movies.
Simple. Easy for techno-dummies like me.

But where to get it? Check google, of course—
Find address. Pull into the parking lot.
Pause. Reconsider. Heart pumping.
Doubts. Questions. Decision-time—
Covid mask on. Open gun shop door. Commitment—
Can they see? Can they tell? Can they fathom?
Can they penetrate my words,
Unveil my true intentions?
To my surprise, a warm greeting—
"Hello! How are you doing today?"
No x-ray eyes. No frowning jury.
Nothing demonically inquisitorial—
Gentle, appreciative, understanding,
Non-judgmental, welcoming, human.
I want a gun. They want my money.

Relieved, I tell them my story—Over 80,
Feel insecure, neighborhood's rowdy, need a pistol.
And then the shock, the let-down—
"Sorry, buddy. Nothing here, out of stock,
Everybody's panic-buying, try someplace else."

Back in the car, deflated,
At a loss, puzzled, wondering—
How, where, when . . . ?
How, where, when . . . ?
How . . . Where . . . When . . . ?
A very personal matter . . .

Beyond the Breakers

Out beyond the breakers
There's an island in the sea.
Wind blows slowly, gently,
Fresh water flows from a spring.
Swaying trees spread shade,
Bear coconuts, bananas, figs,
And when the glorious sun sets,
All the heavens glow in golden light.

Come with me, let us lie on the sand,
Listen to waves and their gentle touch.
Quietude is ours when the sun settles,
Moon glows, stars glisten brightly.
Air, sand, the setting sun, blue night,
Rising moon, all sing so beautifully—

Yes—
        Breathe
        Sigh
Listen quietly—
        Listen . . .
        Hear . . .

We are the songs,
Joyously singing our deepest
Hopes and our highest dreams—
We ourselves are . . .Oh, yes . . .
The life within the music itself!

Lighting the Candle

In the darkest night, so difficult to light the candle.
Difficult to ignore winds rattling the shudders.
Difficult to enter within and feel sanity's soft touch.
Difficult to remember who I am, and rise
Above the madness of these days and times.

The hooded one is with us. We dance
With an invisible partner who clutches us,
Twirls us, sashays us around the world's floor,
His hollow-eyed death-skull laughing at our
Frightened eyes, our tears, our flimsy little masks.

The emotional masks we wore as children
To shield our fragile hearts, doubting minds
And secret shames were very different. Now,
In grocery stores, pharmacies, drugstores,
Post offices—the smell of fear is near.

We dance with death, and the dance won't cease.
Fiddles play madly, drums pound mightily,
Guitars wail, saxophones moan, singers screech,
And death smiles gleefully, leading us on and down
Into this deep dark night, and we can't light the candle.

In the face of insanity—our howls, protests,
Cries in the night, smashed walls, shattered windows,
Gnashing teeth, cringing loved ones, our bellowing,
Our desperate yelling at the wind-tossed sea—
There is no way out, no way to blissful clarity.

But when I close my eyes and see your
Radiant beauty shining within without words,
See your grace, hear your music, and remember
Who I truly am—the silent observer of all that is—
I arise clear-eyed and light the candle once again.

Gone but Still Singing In my Heart-Song

TimBuckleyJeff Buckley
JimiHendrixJanisJoplin
FredNeilOdettaRoyOrbison
RayCharlesLeonardCohen
MartyBalinGeorgeHarrison
JohnDenverHaroldBudd

DaveBrubeckErrollGarnerBillEvans
LennieTristanoCecilTaylor
McCoyTynerRolandKirk
MilesDavisCharlieParker
JohnColtraneCannonballAdderley
DizzyGillespieSonnyStitt
BenWebsterColemanHawkins
JohnnyHodgesLesterYoung
DukeEllingtonBennyGoodman
DjangoReinhardtStephanGrapelli
AstorPiazollaPaulDesmond
GilEvansPaulHorn
ArtPepperStanGetz
GaborSzaboJimHallJoePass

GlennGould
ArthurRubenstein
LeonardBernstein
BachChopinTchaikovsky
RachmaninoffDeBussySatie

WaylonJenningsMickeyNewbury
HankWilliamsJohnnyCash

RogerMillerGeorgeJones
ChetAtkinsDocWatson
ErnestTubbPatsyCline

ErnestHemingwayJackKerouac
SamShepardJimHarrison
JohnSteinbeckEdwardAbbey
HenryMillerWilliamStyron
DostoyevskyThomasMann
HermannHesseNikosKazantzakis
CharlesDickensMarkTwain
EdgarRiceBurroughs

JamesDeanMarlonBrando
RichardBurtonLizTaylor
AvaGardner
LaurenBecallAnnaMangnani
PeterFondaDennisHopper
HarryDeanStantonRobertMitchum
PeterO'TooleT.E.Lawrence

MuhammadAliBruceLee
RobinWilliamsGeorgeCarlin
DudleyMooreJohnnyCarson
GeneKellyGregoryHines
IngmarBergmanFedericoFellini
StanleyKubrick

WilliamShakespeare
JohnKeatsWilliamBlake
WaltWhitmanHenryDavidThoreau
WilliamWordsworthSamuelColeridge
DylanThomasLelandHickman
RobinsonJeffersLewWelch

IsadoraDuncan
VaslavNijinsky
MoriaShearer
MikhailBaryshnikov
RudolfNureyev

OshoKrishnamurti
AlanWattsHenriBergsonColinWilson
SriChinmoyGahlilGibran
BuddhaJesusSosan
GeorgeGurdjieffP.D.Ouspensky
SocratesNietzscheSchopenhauer

LaoTzuChuangTzuLiehTzu
HanShanT'aoCh'ienPoChü-i
LiPoHsiehLing-yünSuTung-Po
IssaRyokanIkkyuKabir

LeonardoDaVinciMichaelangelo
BotticelliVanGoghMonet
ModiglianiWilliamTurner
AlbertBierstadtThomasCole
JacksonPollockFranzKline

KarenHorneyAbrahamMaslow
SigmundFreudCarlJung
AlbertEinsteinSirArthurEddington
RichardFeynmanCarlSagan

MomDadGrandmaGrandpa
AuntJaneAuntEvelyn
CharleneLansingShirleyMitchell
NatashaReatigMaryBrannumCynthiaFischer
CharlieLangdonSteveDeRubyMaggieBelle

Into Light

Into Light

He awakens at five,
Makes his coffee,
Sits for an hour
Bathed in candle light,
Eyes closed, listening,
Being wholly present,
Aware without thought.

In the early morning hush
He walks down the hill
To his beloved studio,
Admiring a cloud-bank
Glowing in pink/gold light,
Silhouetting the ancient live oak
And its sprawling branches.

Enjoying the hour's
Luminous silence, he
Breathes cool air and smiles,
Grateful to be alive.
Closing the studio door,
He sits before his blank-white
Computer screen,
Eyes closed, and waits relaxed,
Waits openly, receptively,
Waits without time . . .

Words emerge like flowers,
Images awaken from within,
A seed sprouts, a leaf springs forth,

A plant grows, slowly ripens,
More flowers open, petals take
Shape, color, form—.

A poem born from emptiness
Into light, sighs, smiles, weeps,
And the cheerful laughter of a
Thousand years spills forth,
Echoing those bright-eyed poets
Who stand together
On the far shore waving,
Smiling, beckoning, calling him,
Welcoming him home
To where the heart is.

I Don't Know Much About God, But I Do Know

She's black, with blue eyes,
Speaks Hebrew, and loves French pastry.
When she turns around,
He's a red-headed, brown-eyed Swede who
Speaks Tibetan with a Peruvian accent.
When he looks to the left,
She's Asian-yellow, 5'9" tall,
And her Icelandic chitchat sounds like Italian.
When she looks to the right,
He's a green-eyed Indian Sikh who
Writes Spanish, and sells real estate in Brooklyn.
When he backflips,
She's a gentle orangutan from Borneo,
With hazel eyes, flowers in her hair,
Thunderclouds and warm rainshowers in her hands.
When she swings on vines,
He's an Arctic polar bear, with blue sky in his eyes,
And all the world's oceans whispering in his ears.
When he playfully slides down a snow-slope,
She's a two-year-old little girl,
With blonde and red and black hair,
Who counts to three in 500 languages,
And cries and laughs in one language that
Mothers all over the world understand.

So what's to know?
Here, have a strawberry dipped in powdered sugar.
God is also delicious!

A Single Candle

Early morning
Pre-dawn light
Silhouetted trees
Birds silent
Dogs sleeping
Windows dark
Dew on parked cars
Chilled air hushed . . .

A single candle
  Lights
The whole world

This Single Radiant Moment

Now an urban recluse,
A kind of affable Zen monk,
I live happily with my wife,
Friend, lover and soul mate—
Not seeking, not searching, not alone,
Not lonely, not aching for wine, women, song,
Or for power, control, ambition, wealth, or fame.

Sitting before a golden candle,
I let thoughts, memories, words
Slow to empty quietude,
Embracing nature's inevitable changes
From youthful ascension to old age,
Inwardly celebrating the fact of life herenow,
Beyond time, noise, distractions, politics, war.

Sometimes in the mind-stream, yes,
I recall this journey's words and music,
The places, laughter, and tears I knew
In my dance through youth, time, and change.

Other times, I simply sit quietly,
Bathed in candlelight,
Mind empty, heart at ease,
Embracing self, no-self, acceptance,
And loving kindness towards
All that is and all that ever has been.

No place to go
Nothing to do
All is well—
Perfect in this
Single radiant moment.

Companions Along The Way

I've always been a stranger in this world,
"Song-seized and wine-wild" in youth,
Discovering mountains, rivers, moons
Almost by accident in my wanderings.

With guitar in hand, I strutted my stuff
In a thousand sleazy dives,
Sometimes on majestic stages, too,
Escaping loneliness in dark bedrooms,
Shadowed bars, lovers' arms,
Music my unfailing friend in every clime.

A stranger wherever I roamed,
I carried certain companions in my suitcase—
The mad ones, at first—Hemingway,
Dostoyevsky, Kerouac and Styron, who
Led me to the aspiring ones
Who sought the light—Frederick Nietzsche,
Alan Watts, Nikos Kazantzakis.

Then a mind-cloud broke
And sunlight flooded in,
Mystifying me, dazzling me,
Opening my eyes to the wonders
Of places and spaces beyond the mind
That no one had touched in me before—
Osho, Krishnamurti, Lao Tzu, Buddha.

Today my companions have become
Those writers and musicians attuned with
Soaring mountains, dashing rivers,
Mirror lakes, quicksilver streams,
Wind in the pines, clear nights, blazing stars,
And lavish moonlight rippling across the tree tops

The quiet profound ones, the ancient ones
Some more than a thousand years old,
Their shimmer-words as fresh today
As early morning sunrises—
T'ao Ch'ien, Po Chü-I, Han Shan.

Between past and present
Rests Eternal Now—
No tomorrow, no yesterday,
No today, no becoming,
No death—just here, just now,
Without thought, movement,
Sound, images, words, or time—
Simply all that's herenow,
Passing through constant change
Within this singing forever-moment.

This Moment

Thought cannot hold this moment,
For this moment
Is not born of remembered yesterdays
Nor leaps into imagined futures.

Here-now
Ends all passing:
Time ceases.

Spacious mind,
Still-point presence—
Without cause, beginning, end,
Thought, division, change.

Contextual presence,
Eternal now:
Radiant, alive,
In this instant's shining silence:

Edges disappear,
Boundaries vanish,
No-mind, no-self, selfless—
Energies merging, flowing,
Forever forming, transforming—
Behold all that is:
Multitudinous creative simultaneity—
Immensity undivided,
Unified,
Infinite,

Holy,
Whole—
And thought cannot contain it.

Cosmic celebration
Spirals, whorls,
Spins, extends,
Unfolds, expands
Within eternal still-point presence—

All is shimmering Light.

The Thinker

There is just too much to think about—
Tons of clutter, rubbish, nonsense
Such as what?
You know, sex, aging, death . . .
What else?
Love, jealousy, anger, time . . .
What else?
Fame, fear, work, money . . .
Anything else?
Everything. . . Nothing . . .

Nothing? You think about
Nothing?
Yes, but the moment I do,
It becomes something
An idea? A concept? Ideology?
Yes, just more rubbish

How about dying to each moment?
What does that mean?
No thought, no past, no future,
No time, no sorrow, just now—
Then what?
Everything becomes new.

Hmmm. Give me a moment—
I need to
Think about that . . .

Five-Thirty

Morning's quietude—

Just over the hill
Freeway traffic
Hissing, murmuring,
A restless ocean—
Fog shrouded trees
Silent in the mist

A raven calls
A thought stirs
A quiet breeze
Sways bamboo

Where, O where,
Rings that distant
  Temple bell?

Wordless Music

Slow rain on the roof
Transports mind-heart to ancient times
No roads, only paths wandering high
Into mountain forests where
Breezes sing through the pines

Thatch-roof huts under towering trees
Quiet meditators sitting still,
Transcending cares, woes,
Disappearing into candlelight

Rain in the here-now,
Transporting mind-heart to ancient times,
Eternity aloft on wings of gentle winds,
The sweet quietude of wordless music

Lost And Found

Those ancient ones,
The Chinese recluses,
The mountain dwellers,
The walking-stick men
Scratching out poems
On granite rocks
        Bamboo stalks
            Fallen trees

Lost and found—
In wilderness—
Cascading waterfalls
Moonlight bathing forests
        Stars glistening in
                Deep black night-skies—

There they were
There they are
There they remain—

Far from thc city's turmoil,
Listening to falling waters
Eyes closed, ears open,
All of heaven and earth
        Dropping into
            Open minds
                Peaceful hearts

Beyond Distinctions

He listened to the songs they sang
And wondered what the secret was:
Melodies danced a spritely jig,
Harmonies waltzed between the lines,
Rhythms danced in swirling waves,
But nowhere could he find the secret.

He listened to moss-covered stones,
To mountain waterfalls cascading into mist;
He studied wind and clouds and felt
Alive within/without, and yet the mystery
Left him wondering, watching, listening
For a door to open, a voice that spoke.

Nowhere could he turn, nowhere ask.
Exhausted, he quit the search, gave up,
Sat under a pine beside a gentle stream,
Let all his questions, words, thoughts,
Concepts and opinions drift away,
Until seeking itself dissolved in air.

In early morning light, a star appeared,
Shining brightly in blue-black skies.
A sense of wonder overwhelmed him—
A sense of flying up and away from self
Into selfless love, timeless beauty,
And nature's astonishing creativity.

Beyond yes and no, beyond distinctions,
Beyond mind's analytical powers
He rose into sourceless light—
No questions, no noise, no effort,
Simple being, like gentle rain on the roof.

Amazed, delighted, humbled, he set forth
Again upon his journey . . . Listening well,
Speaking little, filled with love, peace,
And a sense of wonder shared with all,
He walked quietly, leaving no footprints,
A drifting cloud, floating through air, awakened.

Between Worlds

My home
Is in the mountains
By the sea—
My house
Is in the city
Encircled by
Leaf blowers
Jack hammers
Unceasing traffic—

Between two worlds
I wonder how and why
My bed is here
My heart is there—

Thoughts wandering
Into sheltering glades
Where pines and aspen
Whisper mountain songs
And clear streams
Nourish my aching soul's
          Wild winds

Thou Art That

Your mother cannot help you
Your father cannot help you
Your uncle, friend, lover,
Fox, shark, eagle or dove
        Cannot help you either

You can look to the mountains,
You can look to the sea,
You can look to the sky—
Your gods, demons and saviors
        Remain illusory fabrications

The you you think you are
Must stand alone and see
Mind empty and infinite—disappearing
Into light without darkness, into
        Time without sound or motion

Think on these things
Until questions evaporate and
Thinking itself disappears along with
Desire, envy, fear, greed,
        Anger, cunning, and bitter loss

Vanish into no-mind infinitude
Listen to the silence
See bright light shimmering everywhere,
Without source, direction, purpose—
        Know Thou Art That—rejoice!

Lifetimes

Slanting roof remains sturdy
While falling rain sings inside each drop

Memories float in song,
Some long ago, others only yesterday—

Lifetimes spent wandering, wondering;
A lifetime within each dancing pearl—

Childhood, with adults smiling down;
Adolescence, staring through classroom windows;

College, discovering alcohol and
Psycho-spiritual transportation;

Discovering music, too, dreams,
Sex, power, beauty, stillness;

Discovering books, spinning through history,
Meeting poetry, passion, towering minds.

Sweet rain, music on the roof;
All of my spinning life within each drop.

A single look back contains each smile and sigh;
A galaxy of pictographs, parents, friends, lovers,

Hopes fulfilled; hopes dashed;
Dreams still dreaming while rain

Dances, sings and sways, calling me home
To where the heart abides—

Watching, waiting, wondering . . .

Rising To Light

There are those heroes
        Who leap into the fray,
Raise their gleaming swords high,
        Slay a few dragons,
        Enjoy the applause,
        And disappear into air.

There are others,
        The quiet ones,
Who walk, but leave no prints,
        Whose light shines
        Far and wide
        Bringing peace to all

Between the two
        The world spins in
Creation and destruction—
        Those who rise to light and
        Share love's unitary ways
        Pass through like easy winds

From The Center

Within the vortex,
Unmoving quietude

Encircled by fear,
Ambition, greed,
Hope, strife, loss—
Feeling the anguish, sorrow,
Tears and pain, the rage—

Still and quiet,
A silent mirror reflecting
Those who appear, smile,
Speak, weep, depart—

Life swirling,
Whirling before spirit's
Compassion-eye,
Leaving no dust.

Listen Without Thought

Come walk with me
        Just for a while
Let's leave the city's angry traffic,
        Desperate competition, perpetual noise—
Leave behind our memories, desires,
        And all those ancient fears
Just for a while

Let us walk this dirt road
        To the pond's quiet waters,
Looking at autumn's leaves,
        Seeing their reds and golds;
Listening to the breeze,
        Hearing its music and feeling its
Cool caress on our cheeks

Let us stand beside still waters
        And release the ways
Of mind and time,
        Finding within our quietude
The sights, songs and sounds
        Of life with water, sky, and
Autumn's gentle passing—

Be here for the moment,
        Moving into sound;
Look for a while,
        Learn how to see;
No mind, no time—
        Listen without thought
And hear the inner bell chiming

Recognition

    Suddenly,
Old age crept up,
Bit him from behind,
And Superjock fell,
Surprised, baffled,
Wounded, aching,
This time unable
To rise again and walk—

In that strange moment
Time revealed
Curious wonders—

"So this is the place
My old friends visited
Only yesterday . . .
    Now I know . . .
        Now I know . . ."

Yearning

Where O where are my mountains,
My pure-light Yosemite streams?
How my heartsongs fly to
Towering peaks, mighty pines,
Shadows and quiet places
Where bears wander, eagles soar,
Rainbow trout swim in shady pools
And gentle humans
Walk in reverent wonder.

The Floating Life

Unmoored,
I now stand free
From the self that once was here,
The remembered self,
A dream dreaming itself,
Images of lives lived somewhere else
By someone else with people who once
Were here, now there, now gone . . .

The floating life,
Songs written on water
Cast into mind-sky,
Rising into dimming light,
Vanishing in morning's mist . . .

The Tight-Rope Walker

The tight-rope walker took two
Then three steps from nothingness,
Incandescent inside eternity's shining light
Leaning a bit too far to the left
He almost fell into murmuring memories,
But righted himself lest he disappear
He then leaned a little too far to the right,
And almost phased into dreams
Of fame, love, money, women
Again, he opened his inner eye,
Awakened to present,
Returned to balance—
With empty mind serene,
Aware, open, receptive to
Each nuance, he smiled
And walked slowly onward, alert, alive,
Moving gracefully as a dancer
Within eternity's forever sunrise

Life-Songs

Young white wolf, strong, proud,
Surveying snow-covered forests,
Frosted meadows, icy streams;

Masked Zorro rearing his white horse
Before a setting sun, cape flaring,
Sword pointed skyward, heroic justice aflame;

Buddha meditating, awake, serene,
The worlds within our ten-thousand worlds
Spiral-spinning inside his Kosmic mind—

And so my life-songs swell and sing
In every beat of hummingbirds' wings
And every lover's swooning sigh.

Eat the Cake, Sing the Song

Every New Year another number—
        Yesterday, 2000
        Tomorrow, 2025
        Years ahead, 2040—
All but a moment's flashing dream

This week or two-thousand years ago;
        Today's politics, yesterday's Chinese poets—
        A single moment, embracing all cares,
        Plans, hopes, pain, laughter, joy—
So brightly here, then gone, gone, gone . . .

Live fully? Nothing matters? So what? Yes? No?
        Everything is real. Live in love.
        Eat the cake, sing the song,
        Dance the dance, and when gone comes—
Smile, shine, and lift your candle high

Trust The Process

When critics assail me
For not being what they want,
While failing to understand what I am,
I shed a tear, let them go, move on.

The higher includes the lower;
For the lower is yet ascending.
When the lower breaks through
Into light, love, and unity consciousness,

Understanding arises;
Clarity in lovelight surrounds
The once-wandering innocent;
Harmonious music fills the air.

Love has no divisions, no object,
No time but eternal Now. If
We do not wander astray, how
Can we come home? All is well.

Thoughts come, thoughts go.
We, too, come. We, too, go.
Along the way, we ascend within—
Some slowly, some in a flash—
Let it be. Trust the process.

Three Birds Fly

Across the face of
Morning's full moon

A car passes,
Fades away

Radiant silence

"Don't Just Do Something"

What happens when nothing to say,
Nothing to do, nowhere to go?

Sitting, sitting still, sitting until
Thoughts slow, fade, vanish,
Leaving quiet mind, empty mind,
No-mind bliss like the ancient ones

Whose presence remains in gentle breezes,
In sunlight slanting through the pines,
In midnight candlelight illuminating
Bamboo walls, closed eyes, clear minds

RAIN-SONG

Slow rain, music on the rooftop
Spattering one-two-three

Soon, more rain, pouring down,
Diamonds patter-splashing leaves,
Clouds spreading wings, opening wide,
Torrents loud now, clear, joyous,
Washing all thoughts away
Exuberant rain, orchestral rain,
Rain cleansing the earth, the sky, the mind

And when the rain slows, clouds part,
And sky opens wide and blue

Lo and behold
The rainbow's mighty glory!

The Question Mark

Seeing it all, knowing nothing,
Wandering, wondering, drifting—
An autumn leaf,
A wayward thought,
A broken-hearted lover

Searching beyond the veil
Queries hurled into the void—
From soundless presence,
A chuckle, real or imagined:
A shimmering question-mark

Simultaneity

How strange it seems
Dipping into memory's well,
Looking at the me I was,
The you you were,
The words we spoke in
Joy, wonder, curiosity, love—

How time seemed slow back then—
When will Christmas get here?
Will I ever be 21 and free?
Can't wait for the New Year to arrive.
Anticipation makes time crawl;
Memory retrieves itself instantly.

Meanwhile
Eyes dim; hair whitens;
Foreheads wrinkle; hearing goes;
Joints stiffen; heart weakens,
And we inside can only wonder—
Is this it? Is this the All that is?

What about truth? What about love?
What about understanding? Wisdom?
All those promises — money, happiness,
Well-being, power, profit, prestige,
Knowledge, respect, control, insight,
Awareness, compassion — where?

Maybe time is but a single moment
In which everything in the
Universe happens at once—
Simultaneity in the Eternal Now . . .

When I needed glasses,
I thought clocks were real

The Witness

The Witness never flinches—
        It simply watches
No matter what happens,
        Neither
Yes or no, nor up or down,
Observing rough and smooth,
Tears, laughter, pain, joy,
Watching dispassionately,
With infinite compassion,
Seeing beyond names, titles,
Lust, greed, fear,
Beyond the me, the you,
The gods, demons, scriptures—

The watcher on the hill
Viewing all, seeing all,
Seeing beyond black/white,
Affirmation/negation,
Passions, tastes,
Happiness, misery,
Customs, traditions, laws—

Quiet, non-judgmental,
Present, benevolent,
Aware without opinions,
Without memory,
Without was or will be,
Without time or thought—

The Witness never flinches,
Always present, always with us,
Unchanging, spacious,
Radiant, seeing clearly,
Lighting the way

If we let it . . . If we let it . . .

Three Eyes

With eye of Flesh,
    Embrace all objects, places, processes
That can be seen, measured, touched.
    Caress beauty's rounded shoulder;
Lightly feather-brush
    Monet's water lilies;
Tongue-savor amber
    Chinese honey tea;
Smell sweet roses, rich moist earth,
    Woodsmoke from the campfire;
Listen to Blue Mountain's
    Ripple-streaming waters,
And our lover's timeless bliss-sighs.

With eye of Mind,
    Embrace all words and tales
From India's Vedas,
    Q'umram's ancient scrolls,
Socrates' every question,
    Galileo's telescope,
Goethe's lofty clouds,
    Tolstoy's pen,
Einstein's spiraling number-dreams.

And from eye of Spirit
    Let Buddha's shimmering silence descend,
Lao Tzu's laughter flow,
    Jesus' love envelop us with light,
Osho's wisdom shower flowers,
    And, yes, forevermore

Let Han Shan's quiet simplicity
        Decorate this Blue Mountain cabin
With scented cedar pine boughs,
        Peaceful smiles and
Compassion's sunrise celebration.

Sitting

Without questions
	Without answers
Without future
	Without past
	Without self

Blue sky silence
	Radiant light
Quiet winds
	Music
	In the pines

Nothing

Nothing—
    Infinite potential

Nothing
    Invisible breeze

No time,
    No mind

No mind,
    No time

        Just now,

            Just this,

                Just so

White Without Sound

Feeling the energy,
Loving the dash,
The line,
The sound
The spark

Music in air
Eyes closed,
Sweat streaming
Passionsong
Excitement,
Applause

Suddenly, abruptly
Surprise,
Done
Over,
No mas,
Finished

And now?
Uncomfortable stillness
Quietude unbidden
Anxious rustling

Snow falling silently

White without edges

White without sound

Seasons

Winter snow
Blue in moonlight;
February daffodils
Yellow in sun;
August apples
Sweet in summer's heat;
Red-gold sunbeams slanting
Through autumn's trees—

We do what we can
As well as we can—
Singing, dancing, loving—
Then wave and smile,
And bid a poignant farewell,
Passing the way of all seasons
Even as oceans roar and sigh,
Rolling on
Forever

Yellow Moon, Orange Sun

A flock of geese
Flew across the face of
Of morning's full moon

Flying in a V,
The leader honked once, twice
Yellow moon setting, orange sun rising

Stimulations, Sensations

Stimulations . . . how I loved them
A toke, a drink, a touch, a pill,
Mind whirly-gig-jigging galore

Heavenly pot . . . spiral-rising smoke
So sweet the smell, the taste,
Breathe in, breathe out, relaxation

Alcohol, my Dark Angel . . .
Body warm, humor sailing,
Lust aroused, man-root rising

Touch . . . O skin-touch hot,
Soft and slow, urgent, eager,
Tongue alive, mind lost in cobalt-blue

Acid dreams . . . swirling colors
From anxious separation to
One-with nature, god, infinity

Yes, O yes, how sweet those days of
Mad sensations, stimulations,
Love in the afternoon, beautiful youth.

While Dreams Thrive

Deep-green leaves, yellow lemons,
Not quite ripe, December's song
Cloudy sky, dim morning's light
Perhaps the last cloud, the last day,
The last New Year just over the hill

Easy to dip into regrets
Easy to paint anger, disappointment,
Failure's tears, dashed hopes, nightmare dreams—
If can't forgive, at least forget—

Is this the end of the runway?
The last ditch stand, the big whoopee?
Maybe just a tired sigh, a welcome relief,
Lay down the burden, get on with it?

Poet Lu Yu said, "An old-timer is just a worn-out child,"
That's easy, too, quite flashy, quite true . . .
Wonder if the lemons will ripen before the year turns
Or if the sun will shine, yes, just one more time

Sing the sailor boys home, Ma, let the girls dance,
Swirl their skirts and click heels to music's smile
Let the boys make eyes and light their fires
While clocks spin and dreams thrive . . . no tomorrow

Distant Laughter

High school hallway
Sunlight through far-end window
Glare-shine floor
Watcher watching, wondering

Transparent figures
Locker doors rattling, banging
Blonde hair, pony-tails
Jeans, football jackets

Ghostly figures, dreamlike,
Appearing, disappearing
Shape-shifting, re-appearing
Years ago, long gone

Slowly undulating transparent figures
Doors rattling, far away conversations
Figures shifting, dissolving, re-appearing
Bright-light glare-shine floor

Here, there, unclear, no time
Layered voices, mixed, indistinguishable;
Semi-familiar faces, looking away
Smiles, whispers, distant laughter . . .

Attuned

Following thoughts, tracing moments
No time, looking back, instant recall
Looking forward, dark, unknown
No time in the moment, no looking, no seeking
Rest in the peace of this awakened now

No line back, no line forward, just here, just now
Mind-dreams stream in, stream out, gone
Never were, never is, gone, gone, gone
Wish I were a pussycat, dozing in sunshine
Find home in the empty mind, home in the great All

Nonsense, my friend. Is it? Where, O where, might you
Go to find what's already here? No go, no come,
No Yes, no No, no Maybe, no shift from now
No then, no was, no will be, no time-time-time
Leave it all, be here-now, quiet, still, empty mind attuned

Until Even Looking Disappears

Looking back, the long road to here;
Looking back, the twists, turns, surprises;
Looking back, the ecstatic passions and
Aggressive clawing, climbing, scratching,
Stretching toward higher rungs, needing ever more—

All a dream now, blazing suns, ink-black nights,
For what? To where? These dusty trophies,
These stacks of scrapbooks—smiling ghosts,
Bright-eyed faces, half-remembered names
Lost in River Time, lost and mostly forgotten . . .

And yet—and yet—a kind of liberation—
The sun shines brighter in morning's light,
Radiant with fresh pink and golden clouds;
The wind sounds magically musical, like
Temple bells ringing far away in mountain mists . . .

Looking out was great and often grand—
Looking inward now fills my heart with wonder,
Joy, and infinite gratitude for those remembered
Twists, turns, surprises and ecstatic passions
Floating in mind's shimmering dreamsongs—

Looking inward now, until even looking disappears,
The sense of self and time fade away,
Tranquility descends in golden light,
And, lo, one sees beyond the edge of sight
Into the selfless presence of the shining now . . .

Still Singing

All behind,
        Meaningless now
Memories, dreams,
        Dim flashes through time's mist

Voices, cooing, chattering,
        Yesterday's images,
Ghost-sounds, echoes—
        Passions, angers, loves felt, lost

Memories without substance,
        Hollow repetitions,
Honor them, dismiss them, listen—
        Still singing, so far away

Calling, calling, calling . . .

Rivering

Giving up the personal, the specific, the me-me-me
        Discovering rivering, wet, wild, flowing
Let-go, release, relaxation, sailing
        Sky blue no-mind-vast
Peace, wordless music,
        Wings spreading, soaring,
        Gliding high-wide on river-winds

LIGHT

Glittering water,
Flowing streams, smooth stones,
Warm winds, summer wheat fields,
Light
Tumbling waters
Sparkling diamonds

* * * * *

Light
Without body
Wind without sound
Stirrings without movement
Stillness without center

Far, Far Away

Long flat lake, infinite blue sky
Tucked away, the wandering mind
        Pay no attention

Vague chatterings,
Faint mutterings, shimmering spaces
        Wait, and see . . .

Long flat lake, infinite blue sky

Gathering Light

All is love: no divisions:
Let the dance begin—

Disappear in music:
Vanish in swirls, leaps,
And dancing winds:
Release into herenow All

Ahh, music, sweet music,
How I love thee well and truly.

Time, Age, Change

Flourishing, diminishing
Wondering, watching, waiting
Suddenly, herenow—

Vast quietude

Stones Alive

Looking deeply into mist,
Stones come alive and speak;
Seen clearly in bright light,
Green mountains sway—
Disappearing into timewinds,
One knows how to fly

As we are, we shall never be again

Lovesong

Between passing cars,

The song of an owl

Calling its mate:

"Ooo-whee,

Ooo, ooo, ooo . . ."

Sing Me A Song, Ma

Stomach growling
Lights dimming
Sounds muffled
Body aching
  And yet . . .

Light grows
Ever-brighter
Compassion,
Ever-stronger
  Love
Ever-deeper . . .
  Wider . . .
  Truer . . .

Sing me a song, Ma,
My legs can't
Carry me further . . .

Mergence

He whacked me with his words,
        Pierced me with his arrow-eyes,
Threw me down with his tone,
        And hoped to leave me desolate.

I became a transparent cloud
        Vacant, cool, unresisting,
Floating, receptive,
        Embued with living light.

His eyes and voice grew soft;
        His arrows vanished inside light;
We merged our separate musics—
        And, lo, a new life was born.

Gone Beyond

Getting ready to go
Can feel it now
Packing bags
Imagining isolation
Scribbling a few words
Shutting down computer
Closing front door

World on fire
Friends dying, dead, vanished
Strange streets, angry traffic
Jackhammers, leaf blowers, sirens—
Wandering without purpose,
Distant memories echoing
Childhood's darkland laughter

Gone, not to the store
          Gone, not to the park
          Gone, not to heaven—
"Gaté . . . Gaté . . . Gaté . . ."
Gone . . . Gone . . . Gone—

          Gone utterly beyond

The Luminous Now

When not aware,
My life goes on without me

Sleep, precious sleep—
  And then—

Seeing without mind-dreams
Between self and what is

How bright the light,
Awake, aware, alert

Attuned to the ever-shifting
  Luminous Now.

Beyond The Search

Searching for love, passion,
Whispers, sighs?
For moans, groans,
Gasps and muted cries?
For kisses, lips, tongues,
Strokes, swoons,
Nipples, pussy, cock?

What about delightful visual sensations—
Photos, television, films, videos?
Spectacular swordplay, gun fights,
Car wrecks, murders, wars, and wild fires?

What about laughter, tears,
Hope, disappointment, drama,
And the right/wrong, yes/no violence
Of opposites clashing everywhere?

And yes, O yes, how about
Wailing guitars, thundering drums,
Dancing feet, swiveling buttocks, and
Swirling bodies reeling in dazed ecstasy?

What about knowledge, language,
Literature, philosophy, poetry?—
Maybe searching for quirky,
Wine-seized dazzle-words?—
What about those song-wild,
Sweet-soft, loud-fast, mad-dash,
Hurley-girly, brain-igniting,

Heat-rising, linguistic
Whoopee-do word-flames?

Maybe the search is for
Money, power, control,
Wealth, and fame enough
To fill that aching void inside—
Can diamonds, furs, yachts,
Boats, cars, hotels, airplanes,
And endless sex ever
Satiate that hunger for a love
The father never gave?
For a respect that never came?
Can "Me, Mine, and More"
Ever fill that horrideous maw?
Can inner strength ever
Spring from money, power,
Greed, sycophantic slaves,
And ten thousand glittering toys?

Perhaps now the search has
Become a gentler seeking—
For mountains and rivers,
Deserts and oceans,
Quiet streams, still lakes,
Forests among mist clouds.
No questions, no answers,
No desperate competition,
Grasping desire, fearful clinging,
No egoic fire, fun, fury—
Just quietude among the singing pines,
Radiant stillness in a loving heart,
Inner spaciousness and
Beauty of body, mind, spirit.
Could that be?

Maybe by now the search
Itself has been transcended, yes?
Dropping the search, dropping future—
No longer seeking sensations,
Distractions, escape, knowledge,
Power, wealth, control, notoriety.
No longer perceiving nature's
Opposites as "violently clashing,"
But as complementary unities,
Perfectly balanced in natural harmony.

Not looking at yesterday's triumphs,
Or tomorrow's ambitious dreams,
Or tradition's Bibles, Korans, and Gitas,
But awakening in quietude, inner peace,
And inclusive, compassionate selflessness.
Maybe discovering a vibrant here-now
Beyond seeking, doing, becoming.
Realizing love, understanding and clarity
Within nature's relentless changes.

Perhaps not searching and seeking,
But simply sitting quietly, deeply relaxed,
Wholly merged with existence,
Embracing self and all peoples,
Blessing the flowers, the animals,
And all of the stars throughout the heavens.

Perhaps now you find yourself
Well beyond mind-time, yes—
Standing with clear eyes open, yes,
In the forever-moment of this
Shining here-now instant,
Happy, healthy, whole and holy—
Yes . . . O, yes . . . yes!

Go Gently

Go gently into that good night.
Do not rage against the dying of the light.
Nor haste, nor flight, nor fight,
But sweetly, lovingly, embrace

Those fleeting moments, the setting
Of the sun, its light and beauty,
Its astonishing grace and grandeur,
The radiance of our shining center.

Relax, let go the fear; release resistance.
The sunset's red-orange hues shine
Before our inner eye, majestic, elegant—
Nature's eternally impassioned finale.

This radiant inner silence is
Our own life's crescendo: the beatitude
Of nature's glory in beams of
Golden-red and silver luminescence.

Release the heart's fearful No. Step into serenity.
Sweetly embrace quietude, this moment's bliss.
Time is timeless here and now, infinite presence, yes—
Open your eyes and treasure your golden light.

Here for a while, we dance, sing, aspire, make love—
So intense our time, so beautiful, wondrous,
Exciting, glorious . . . Cherish it now and go gently,
Bravely, into that serenity-light forever.

The Land of Light

With my words,
I gave my heartfelt all
Exploring dark valleys,
Reaching high peaks,
Arriving at those inner spaces
Where clouds clear,
Mists part ways,
And ancient mysteries reveal
Themselves completely.

Awareness, compassion,
Insight and love's embrace
Imbued those lines as I
Danced with wind,
Dove into dark waters,
Flew into vast blue skies,
And embraced past, future,
And the joy of Eternal Now.

Some were ready to receive,
Immediately grasping
The inner sense of those
Non-repressive,
Non-ideological,
Non-dogmatic
Thoughts speaking of
Of joy-light, inner peace,
And radiant understanding.

Those who could,
Understood and appreciated,
And joined me in living
Our heartsong's timeless joys.
They entered with me
Into the land of light
Where the ancient ones
Greeted us with smiles and blessings,
Joy-light shining in their eyes.

Those who could not see clearly
Remained second-hand souls,
Walled within borrowed knowledge,
Conventions, customs, codes,
And socially conditioned minds.
They spouted protestations,
Citing rules, guidelines, distinctions,
And philosophical "twisty thoughts"
That protected them from
The truth of themselves and others.
They chose instead
The forever-miseries of
Tradition, repetition, analysis,
Ambition, politics, religion,
And the corrosive greed of
Me-Mine-and More.

What I said was not what they heard.
What they heard was not what I said.
Blinded by what they thought they knew,
Their ignorant rejections
And arrogant criticisms

Generated surprise in me at first,
Followed by profound disappointment—
Limping and stumbling in the
Darkland sorrows of my aching heart,
That disappointment troubled me
Until I eventually realized—

No one can escape
Their cherished ignorance and
Resistance to evolutionary development
Until they themselves find their heart
Ready and willing to take that upward leap
Into bright-light psycho-spiritual realization
And the wholeness of being at-one-with All.
Acceptance, patience, understanding, and love
Make all the difference—

Are we conscious? Are we asleep? Are we snoring?
Are we open, receptive, aware and
Appreciative enough to transcend
Our conditioned feelings and hypnotized thoughts?
Can we grow up beyond
Distinctions and argumentation?
More importantly: Can we wake up to love and joy
And their celebratory, unifying powers?

Some, yes.
Some in time.
Some never—

No golden gods,
No Halleluyah saviors.

Meanwhile, I can share with others
Only what I have become.
After more than eight decades,
I stand as one who finally sees clearly
The joys and sorrows we humans create.
Not a pretty sight—horrors abound—
Yet we are also radiant with creative energy that
Yearns for awakening, for realization, for fulfillment.
Aspiration, strength, and immense possibility
Exist as one in the heart of the rose.

As works in progress,
We arrive, we strive, we struggle, we hope—
With luck and skill, we transcend ignorance,
Growing into wholeness, sharing with
Receptive others whatever light, love and joy
We discover within ourselves.

Bless the Gentle Ones.
They lead the way.

May their strong arms
Hold the lanterns high.

Forever-Song

Speak, my heart.
        My heart is your heart.
Listen, my heart.
        My attention is your attention.
Be with me, beauteous voice,
        Drift with me,
        I am with you.

With Special Thanks To

Influential Poets

Tao Ch'ien, Hsieh Ling-yün,
Han Shan, Li Po,
Stonehouse,
Po Chü-I, Lu Yu

And Immortal Luminaries

Buddha
Lao Tzu
Osho
J. Krisnamurti

About The Poet

Lee Underwood's poems have appeared in two published books, entitled *Timewinds* and *Diamondfire*, as well as in several journals, including "Light of Consciousness," "ZamBomba," and "In The Grove." His latest work, *Into Light*, is a series of higher-consciousness poems nearly all of which were written in 2020.

During the late '60s and early '70s, Underwood played lead guitar with singer/songwriter Tim Buckley on seven of the nine albums Buckley released while alive, including *Happy Sad* and *Starsailor*. Underwood also appeared on several posthumous Buckley CDs, notably *Dream Letter: Live in London 1968* and *Works In Progress*. He toured America and Europe with Buckley for seven years, and in 2001 published a book entitled *Blue Melody: Tim Buckley Remembered* (Backbeat; San Francisco).

While living in Los Angeles in the '70s and '80s, Underwood wrote extensively about music and musicians. His articles, interviews and reviews appeared in dozens of periodicals, including *Down Beat* (West Coast Editor, 1975-1981), *L.A. Times, L.A. Weekly, Rolling Stone, Pulse, Jazz Forum, L.A. Free Press, New Realities, Body/Mind/Spirit, New Age Journal,* and many others.

He co-authored flutist Paul Horn's autobiography, *Inside Paul Horn* (HarperCollins; 1990), and in 1991 received the Crystal Award for Music Journalism at the NAM Convention in Hollywood.

Underwood graduated from San Francisco State College with a degree in English and World Literature and briefly attended graduate school at UC Berkeley. He and his beloved wife, Sonia Crespi, live in Petaluma, CA.

Website: http://www.leeunderwood.net

www.ingramcontent.com/pod-product-compliance
Lightning Source LLC
LaVergne TN
LVHW090957080826
845145LV00003B/1039

* 9 7 8 1 6 3 6 4 9 6 9 8 6 *